The
Teachers
Alphabet Book

The **Teachers** Alphabet Book

Joseph Cornacchioli

The Teachers Alphabet Book - 2009
Photos used with permission from users of www.sxc.hu/
Y Photo by Julia Freeman-Woolpert
No part of the publication may be reproduced or photocopied at anytime.
ISBN# 1441410589

www.josephcorn.com

ABCDEFG...
See How Exhausting Teaching Can Be!

A is for Apple

What suck-ups give
the teacher.

Alice gave her teacher an *apple* everyday.

Unfortunately, her teacher was allergic to apples.

B is for Bell

That annoying noise that goes off every 43 minutes or so.

Betty became an elementary school teacher so she didn't have to hear the *bell* that signals to change class.

Instead she deals with crying children.

C is for Class

Love or hate them,
you get a new one every year.

Connor never liked his *class*.

Soon Connor realized he just didn't like children.

D is for Dance

What the school has for
every event.

David never wanted to chaperone a school *dance*. It brought back bad memories from his childhood.

E is for Essays

Tell the students they have
to write one and listen
to them complain.

Erica never gave her students *essays* because she didn't want to have to read all of them.

F is for Food Fights

Don't get caught in the middle.

Frank is a teacher.

Frank started a *food fight*.

Frank isn't a teacher anymore.

G is for Grading

What you do
nights and weekends.

Gina hated *grading* tests so she gave all of her students A's.

When the state test came around the students were in for a surprise.

H is for Homecoming

A lot of hype for
a football game.

Heath couldn't get any lessons done during *homecoming* week.

I is for Irritated

Teachers never get irritated...

Irina got *irritated* everyday by her student who farted in class.

J is for Junk Food

Sugar = Bad

Jimmy's class had *junk food* everyday for snack. By 1pm the entire class crashed from their sugar high and had naptime.

K is for Kids

Teaching brings out
the kid in you.

Kathy teased the *kids* in her class.

Kathy is the teacher.

Kathy is going back to school to change professions.

L is for Lockers

Where the students are always hanging out.

Lance had to help freshman out of *lockers* daily.

M is for Mondays

Yuck!

Meredith loves *Monday's*....now that she's retired.

N is for Naptime

Something you will want daily.

Nicole made sure her class had *naptime* every day.

Nicole taught 10th grade.

O is for Opposite

What is the
opposite of opposite?

Olga thought she knew what her students would do next, then they did the complete *opposite*.

P is for Paychecks

What you get every other Friday!

Patricia spent her entire *paycheck* on supplies for her class.

Q is for Quiet

Something your class never is.

Quincy occasionally wore earplugs in class, because his students were never *quiet*.

The only downside was he never heard the student's questions.

R is for Running

Hope you're in good shape!

Robert got in trouble for *running* in the halls...he is the principal.

S is for

Student Teachers

Who wants one?

When Sara was a *student teacher* she fell asleep during a math lesson. Now she fears teaching any math.

T is for

The Teachers Lounge

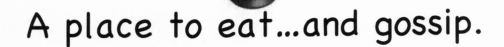

A place to eat...and gossip.

Tim never went to *the teachers lounge* because he felt outnumbered by all the female teachers.

U is for Uncertain

Who knows?

Teachers are always *uncertain* of what will come every September, but every spring they are sad and happy another year has ended.

V is for Virus

Cover your mouth.

Valerie wore a mask in her class whenever there was a *virus* going around.

He students laughed at her.

W is for Work

What you do....everyday.

Will never thought of teaching as *work*, he thought it was fun!

X is for X-Axis

The opposite of the Y-Axis.

Xavier would always confuse the *x-axis* with the y-axis when teaching math.

His students didn't do well on the state math test.

Y is for Yelling

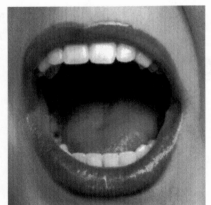

This will happen a lot in class.

Yolanda never wanted to be the teacher who was always *yelling*.

Her anger issues prevented that.

Z is for Zoo

What your classroom looks like.

With all the sounds and excitements coming from Zach's class, you could have sworn it was a *zoo*.

Now You Know Your ABC's
Next Time Won't You Teach With Me?

abcdefgh
ijklmnopq
rstuvwxyz